How to Pay for College with Grants & Scholarships

By Alicia R. Peters

© A. R. Peters 2023

How to Pay for College with Grants and Scholarships

Copyright, A.R. Peters, 2023

All Rights Reserved. No part of this publication may be reproduced, stored in a retrieval system, or transmitted in any form or by any means, ---electronic, mechanical, or photocopy, recording, or any other except for brief quotations, for promotional purposes, not to exceed 400 words, without the prior permission of the publisher.

First published in 2023 by A.R. Peters

Sturbridge Square, Hayman Company

1488 Westford Circle

Building C, Suite #205

Westlake, OH 44145

ISBN # (eBook)

ISBN # (paperback)

Cover Design by ----Valentina P.@ vikiana (Hired her on Fiver.com)

Foreword by Dr. Carl A. Collins Jr.

Book Description by Tammytypesonfiver (Hired her on Fiver.com)

No part of this book may be reproduced by any mechanical, photographic, or electrical process, or in the form of a phonographic recording; nor may it be stored in a retrieval system, transmitted or otherwise copied for public or private use, other than for 'fair use' as brief quotations as brief quotations embodied in articles and reviews, without prior written permission of the publisher.

For permission requests, write to the publisher "permissions" at peters_alicia@icloud.com

The information in this book should not be treated as a substitute for legal, financial, or investment advice, and should never be used without first consulting with a professional to determine what my be best to determine your company or personal business needs.

The publisher and the author do not make any guarantee or other promise as to any results that may be used or any other contents of this book. Examples in the book are independent and genuine. However, they do not guarantee or represent a warranty of similar results.

This book is devoted to the 679,000 students in the United States who dropped out of institutions of higher learning during the Coronavirus Pandemic. May you find solace within these words and complete your education with the information found on these pages.

Table of Contents

Foreword 1

Introduction 3

Federal Funding 7

State Funding 13

Institution Scholarships 17

Other Academic Financial Aid (That Did Not Work Out for Me) 21

Grants & Scholarships I Received That Did Not Pertain to Getting a Degree 25

Other Social Programs I Used 29

How to Know if a Grant or Scholarship is Right For You 31

Conclusion 33

Gratitude 35

References 37

Foreword

I met the author of this book while we were attending classes at a state university. Alicia was a full-time student working on her baccalaureate degree in psychology. I was attending law school classes at night. During our conversations Alicia discovered that I had already earned a master's in business administration. Medical Doctorate and a Ph. D. in semi-conductor physics. Alicia decided that with my experience in earning two doctorates and before them an MBA, I might be an ideal person to assist her in her educational pursuits as her Academic Advisor.

I have continued to advise her and even encouraged her to get her own master's in business administration. Alicia has used her logic and understanding of the finances needed to pay for her schooling to explain as much to other students how they too can help gain finances for their collegiate degree searches.

I now have a full grant to pay for my Law School tuition at the same University wherein I received my two doctorates. My former University had an annual practice of enlisting present and past students to call alumni of the school to garner pledges to the University's endowment funds. I had been very successful in getting financially capable former students to contribute to the endowment fund and I had discovered that the tax code of the IRS allowed for anyone to pay for any student's tuition and expenses as long as the student recipient was identified, and the funds went directly to the school. For that contribution, the donor could receive a dollar-for-dollar deduction on the donor's federal income taxes on the following years tax return.

This information caused many former alumni that I solicited during the "Telethon" donation petition to make very large contributions to the University. Since the particular alumni who I had donated request to have their donations identified as person I had spoken with, it became very clear to the organizers of the Telethons that I had participated in earning the University thousands of dollars and in some years around a million dollars. As a reward for being able to initiate these very large donations, I was awarded a full scholarship grant to earn my law degree at the school from which I had already earned two degrees.

Alicia has identified in this book that a tax deduction by any person, related to a student or not, can be earned by the donor as the donation has been made directly to the school and as long as the student is specifically named. This full tax deduction for a donation to a student's educational costs is just another method that can help a student to earn a degree with donated or granted money.

I believe Alicia has used her own experience to put together a compendium of information that will guide and assist any person who wishes to gain help in paying for their college tuition. I am very proud that I have been a good friend and a resourceful Academic Advisor to a person who will be making her influence felt widely not just in this book, but in all of her future endeavors.

Carl Collins, MBA, MD, Ph.D., and soon to be L.D.

Introduction

First, thank you for buying my book. As I write this, it says on my LinkedIn profile that I am a skilled grant and scholarship writer, self-employed, and a full-time student. I receive inbound messages from companies and individuals asking me if I can write a grant proposal for their project all the time. I am constantly turning down work. I am about two classes away from completing my MBA. Before I did this, I worked in sales in the beauty industry. I achieved success with the accounts I managed, often ranking number one in the region, district, or, on one occasion, even the country. This required a relevant skill to becoming a successful writer: persuasive communication.

After doing everything I could in the beauty industry and affiliate wellness and fitness businesses, I decided to go back to school full time at the ripe age of thirty-seven. I was determined to get a bachelor's degree because I kept hearing that I needed one. I did not understand that. I already knew everything about the business and was remarkably successful, but one company that I wanted to work for would not hire me without that piece of paper. If you have experienced a comparable situation or are determined to get an education and get it paid for, keep reading.

My parents never set aside any money to put me through college. Both had a very old-school mentality. My mother never finished college. My father put himself through night school with his G.I. Bill from the Navy. They never asked me what I wanted. I had to figure it out myself. One of the results is the book you are reading now.

My hope is that this book inspires you to get the money you need for your education or any other project. Inside this book are some tips and skills I have acquired while in school that have done just that for me. Sometimes, in the past seven years, I have received money from making a phone call or drafting an email. As of this writing, I have received over $92,000 from grants and scholarships and another $36,000 in gifts and cash for living expenses. I am currently applying for a Fulbright Grant, which will allow me to study overseas for a year while earning my doctorate and writing my dissertation. I have also made income in other ways from writing, but that is for another book.

Sometimes I asked for it, and sometimes people saw my potential and gave it to me. I want to be completely transparent with you. An important reminder is that I *decided* to make this my career. I knew this was what I wanted. I put "decided" in italics in that last sentence because that word means "to kill off any other possibilities." I knew I wanted to pay for college this way, so as I went through my academic career full time, I always kept my eyes and ears peeled for new opportunities for grants and scholarships. I was constantly working on at least one grant and one scholarship application.

I had no idea what I was doing when I started. I did not have a book like this. As soon as I turned in an application, I started researching another. Having an accountability partner at the beginning, which I highly recommend, helped establish good habits. Having someone holding you accountable makes a world of difference. I recommend this whenever you are trying to reach a big goal. My friend Angela and I would start every day by sending each other our daily to-do lists. We would email each other the actions we were taking to forward the grant or scholarship application we were working on. Even small actions—one email, one phone call, one form to fill out, or one paragraph per day—add up. If you make the same commitment, you can accomplish what I did: your tuition, books, and living expenses can all be paid for. Do a little every day to avoid feeling overwhelmed.

Spend the rest of your time focused on schoolwork, class, applying for that coveted internship with the dream company you want, or other activities you enjoy.

I had been working for other people and companies full-time for over twenty years, and I knew I would not be able to do that if I wanted to get through school quickly and at full-time status. With that in mind, it is pertinent to know that some of the techniques I used worked because I was a full-time student. I noticed that I received a lot more money when I was dedicated to my education full time. Being a grant and persuasive writer is an in-demand career. If you fall in love with it, as I have, it can be a marketable skill for a lucrative career that will allow you to work from wherever you want, whenever you want. The most important thing I want you to remember in grant and scholarship writing or application is that if you do not ask for the money or do not apply, they will not give it to you.

I have broken down the funding I received into three parts: federal, state, and local institutions. I have received money from private sources as well. Federal funding comes from the U.S. government or your country. State funding comes from your state of residence, in my case, Ohio. There is also county funding, which is how I received my medical coverage and food allowance. The local funding will be from the institution where you are registered to take classes. Other funding opportunities exist. While I have never received funding from my city or an independent nonprofit organization, I have received gifts that were related to one of these other funding sources. You have to have a personal relationship with these foundations. Below, I will tell you exactly how I received all of the funding I did. Most of it has to do with persuasive communication, believing in yourself, and determination. Anyone can do it.

Federal Funding

Federal Pell Grant

Everyone receives Federal Pell Grant money from their Financial Application for Federal Student Aid (FAFSA) until they complete a bachelor's/baccalaureate degree if they fill out a FAFSA form. This amount is based on your or your family's income from *two years* ago. It is also not based on what your family *actually* contributes to your education. Has either of your parents changed jobs in the past two years? Have your parents gotten divorced? Have you moved to another geographical income area? Most importantly, are your parents giving you money for your education? Depending on the answer to any of these questions, your estimated family income contribution (EFICC) may be incorrect.

*An important note to mention here: My status was *independent* as a full-time student. Your status can be declared *independent* if you live on your university campus or have a *separate address* from your parents.

On the first page of your *Student Aid Report*, the EFICC number is about a third of the way down the first page (at the time that I am writing this). If this number is not zero, and you are at full-time status, your first action is to go to your institution's financial aid office and appeal it. This is an important first step. It is the difference between receiving a few hundred dollars for your Federal Pell Grant or thousands of dollars per academic school year.

What that looks like in real life is that you walk into the financial aid office with your *Student Aid Report*. I suggest printing it out and not having it pulled up on your phone. You never know if the Wi-Fi signal will work. Depending on the size and policies of your institution, you may have to make an appointment. Be sure that you are speaking with someone who is a seasoned employee in the financial office to get the intended results. Tell them assertively that you want to appeal your EFICC amount. If they do not know how to do that, you are talking to the wrong person. Keep asking until someone knows how to show you through the process. There is going to be a form to fill out. When you get to the part where they ask how much your family contributes to your education, you respond with $0.

At the time of this writing, I am in the 2023–24 school year. I Googled the answer to the following question: "How much money can a full-time student get from a Federal Pell Grant right now?" The answer was $7,395 (studentaid.gov). It goes up every year due to inflation. If you are not getting at least this amount, appeal your EFICC number again until the number on your Student Aid Report says $0. This amount is distributed throughout the school year every semester. The reason I did not know what the number was is that I am in graduate school. You will not get this amount in Federal Pell Grant money once you complete your bachelor's/baccalaureate degree, so milk that cow as much as you can. If possible, do this in high school for up to two years before entering a higher education institution. Do this every time you fill out your FAFSA form, which will be every academic year around October. It will set you up for the following school year. Make sure your EFICC number is $0. I was granted $22,290 for my education thanks to this one way of receiving grant money. You can get more!

*Important note: Another factor is that you must register at a *regionally accredited institution*. These institutions transfer credits to other regionally accredited institutions because they have the same standards. If you are unsure, call the institution you are considering applying to, have applied to, or have already been accepted to. This is particularly important if you want to further your education beyond an associate degree.

If you are committed to your education full time, will you be making the same amount of income that you made two years ago? Probably not. If you are, more power to you. I know I would burn myself out if I did. If I worked full time and went to school full time, I would not get through college. You may receive opposing opinions about this. I chose to ignore those people. They never offered to support me through school, so if you have an opposing viewpoint, consider the source. Are they as devoted to your education as you are? Not likely. This is an unconventional way to put yourself through school, but there are multiple ways to do everything. There are tons of grant and scholarship money out there that go untapped every year.

Supplemental Education Opportunity Grant (SEOG)

There is nothing to do besides what I have described above to receive this grant. This money was granted to me exactly two years after I started as a full-time student. Why did I receive it? This is likely because I kept my income (the amount I claimed on my taxes) as low as possible, and I was considered independent from my parents. I maintained full-time status for two years. It could have been a combination of all three of these situations. I will take it! I received $400 in grant funding. You may think, "That's not that much money." But it was free and required zero effort. I will take it.

(Your State of Residence) College Opportunity Grant

This is a state-funded grant, so it is different for every state. I received this by filling out the FAFSA form and following the steps above. No other action is needed. I received it in my third year, when I entered my bachelor's/baccalaureate program. I received $2,000 in grant funding.

Federal CARES Act Grant (Coronavirus Aid Relief and Economic Security)

I was "lucky" enough to be enrolled as a full-time student when the global pandemic occurred because of the coronavirus, otherwise affectionately known as COVID-19, or The Great Resignation. If you are "lucky" enough to have this status during an economic crash, as I was, the federal government will reward this behavior. During economic slides, which happen every four or five years, the government often pumps money into the economy, so if you are working on at least a bachelor's/baccalaureate degree, there is a good chance an economic crash will happen during your academic tenure. At first, I received money through my FAFSA form again.

But the coronavirus kept persisting, affecting not only myself but also the institutions I was attending and their employees. This money softened the blow. I kept calling the financial aid office and asking for additional funding. An effective way to keep an eye on this is to read your institution's newsletter, as they often update students on how to receive relief funding in an emergency. Any time you are running out of money to pay for college, this is an emergency. The worst thing they can say is that they do not have the funds, but every institution has an emergency fund. They claimed that they were being issued additional funding by the federal government, but it would be distributed through the institution. The amount they would receive was based on enrollment and need, so they were glad I called and expressed a need. They put me on a waiting list to receive grant funding. Again, this only took a phone call. If I saw the funding slowing down, I would call again to see if I were still on the list. This moved me to a higher priority. With this little bit of persistence, I received $10,033, in about $2,000 increments, in grant funding (irs.gov, 2023).

Coronavirus Response & Relief Supplemental Appropriations Act (CRRSAA)

This was a $14 billion grant relief fund created by the federal government after the first CARES Act grant funding ran out. I had to ask for it and be persistent toward my institution's financial aid and Student Services offices. They got to know me very well. I received $3,081.25.

Higher Education Emergency Relief Funds (HEERF)

There are three tiers of distribution for this grant based on priority. It is important to continue following up when grant money is distributed in this way during an economic crisis. If you hear about a grant, do a Google search to see when the distribution times are. They usually have windows. This action will move you to a higher priority if you follow up. I received $1,656 for this grant. The maximum amount that a student is supposed to receive is $900 per academic term. It is pertinent to know the number you want to ask for and do your research before you make a follow-up call to the financial aid office or student accounts, so you can ask for the maximum amount. Keep on following up. Put reminders in your calendar to do so. When you follow up, ask them when the next distribution time is.

* Important note: Over 679,000 students across America withdrew from college and did not return the following year (Krupnick, 2022). If students were aware of this funding, I wonder how many would still be in school or would have completed their education. It also makes me wonder how this will impact the economy in the future.

*Another important note is that I was already used to taking classes online and had the skillset to work independently for a few years before this occurrence. I can only imagine that this was one of the reasons why so many students dropped out of school. They did not have this skillset or structure in place and were tasked with not getting the mentorship and one-on-one attention they needed.

As you can see, this book is being written post-pandemic, and we are now dealing with the aftermath. The workforce has been reformulated around working remotely. Many companies have tried and failed to adapt to this business model and are losing great employees. Working remotely is more economical for the workforce, and it enables students to make money while going to school by receiving grants and scholarships. See the **Distance Learning Scholarship** section for more information on this subject.

State Funding

(Your State of Residence) Means Jobs Grant

This was the first time I was introduced to a grant. I chose to apply for grants and scholarships because I was injured in my previous position and wanted something that was not as labor-intensive. I was a displaced worker who had severe back and neck pain, needed knee surgery, and did not have health insurance. My previous employer had gotten their health insurance plan eliminated due to the Affordable Health Care Act. It did not fulfill the minimum requirements required by this act. I was in a car accident too and had "luckily" received $5,000 in bodily injury money to apply toward my health care needs. However, this was not the grant.

    I did physical therapy in an indoor pool at a local church. While there, I started talking with another woman who was a librarian. Hint: Librarians can be a great resource for grants and scholarships. More on them later. She told me about this grant, which would pay for the last year of your associate degree through the state. I called this organization to set up an appointment the next day. They have nearby centers in every state. If you live in a rural area, it is possible to take a workshop and do the work for the grant online. Since the pandemic, they now offer online services and classes. First, I was required to attend a three-day workshop. This workshop was specifically for displaced workers like me. It also pertained to people who had been laid off from their company, not only injured workers who were in rehabilitation programs.

The workshop consisted of resume writing, interview questions, and a skills placement test, which they send to employers to show your strengths. They set me up with a case worker, who drilled me on interview questions and critiqued my resume after I had been through the workshop. They also have job placement, but I was not looking for that yet. I communicated again that I was in school full time and interested in the grant available for full-time students to pay for their last year of college to complete their associate degree. She did not communicate this, but her actions showed that this was not her specialty. She ended up transferring to another office. When I tried to follow up with her, I was not getting anywhere.

This is where my persistence and persuasive communication came in. After months of not hearing from her and not getting approved for a grant or being told of any additional steps, I asked to speak with her supervisor. I explained the situation to this woman. She finally reassigned me. Because of my previous experience, she assigned me to someone who aggressively pushed through my grant application. I had two meetings in person with this new grant counselor, and within a month, I received approval for $6,000 in tuition. In addition, they assigned me to someone who managed my grant, a third-party partner of the institution I attended. Her job was to be sure I had all the materials needed for my classes, such as expensive Texas Instrument calculators for math classes. This woman became an ally of mine in times of distress.

This grant also connected me with another non-profit organization called PCs for People. They provided me with refurbished computers that were returned to factory settings and had updated software. It cost me nothing and was included in my grant. I just had to go pick it up. My name was already in their system. I had an account created when I arrived at their facility. While at PCs for People, I discovered that they offered tech support for the duration of my grant. It has continued while I have been a full-time student. They also provided a government-sponsored Wi-Fi hotspot and free internet access, which I must renew monthly. Before this, I was paying over $130 per month for Best Buy to maintain my computer and over $60 per month for my Wi-Fi and internet access. I was relieved of those two bills. It saved me so much money during my academic tenure. I would recommend looking into PCs for People's availability in your state. When I drafted this book, PCs for People was available in twenty-nine states and was expanding. They also offer refurbished computers to the public for reasonable prices based on your income, which is why they cater to college students. Go to pcsforpeople.org to check it out.

Opportunities for (Your State Residence) with Disabilities

This grant may or may not be available to everyone because not everyone has a disability. I get it. But I did not know that I had a disability before I looked into this grant. I have a minor mental disability that is managed and was still approved for this grant. I had to produce medical records and fill out a form. I originally started pursuing this grant because I was a displaced worker. I had to prove that I had a disability with medical records. Hint: You can get approved for this if you have documented proof of seeing a psychologist regularly. Your psychologist and your grant counselor, once you are assigned to one, can provide this documentation for you. Seeing a psychologist is excellent for self-reflection, which can be a functional way of navigating the academic arena if you are interested in and committed to your personal growth. Your psychologist will have to document a diagnosis anyway to get you approved through your medical care provider for ongoing psychological appointments, even if you do not have anything wrong with you. I have been consistently seeing a psychologist for almost seven years. It has been part of my support system throughout college.

In addition to receiving $8,676 to complete my bachelor's/baccalaureate degree, I also received gas cards at Speedway gas stations. I had to document how much I was driving to receive these funds. This money was approved by a partner organization called the Vocational Rehabilitation Agency. This foundation also has job placement for one year from your graduation date. Since I decided to do a graduate program, I simply closed my case, and I can reopen it when I am ready to reenter the workforce.

This was another scenario in which I was initially placed with a grant counselor that did not meet my needs. I ended up having to request a different counselor. It is okay to do this if you are not getting your needs met. This is the case with any type of relationship.

She asked me what I wanted to do when I graduated. Be prepared with an answer that is an economic need. What I mean by this is that these types of foundations are looking to put their money into people who can fill gaps in the marketplace. I knew there were a lot of human resources positions available. This may require a chat with your academic counselor or a Google Search: "What are the most in-demand jobs in the U.S. market right now?" Keep this in mind when applying for any grants or scholarships. If you have a clear goal, you are more likely to get approved if it fills a need in the marketplace.

Institution Scholarships

Distance Learning Scholarship

I received this scholarship because an academic counselor encouraged me to take an online class. Only listen to your academic counselor if it serves your purpose, not theirs. Thanks to this recommendation, I took two classes online, and it worked better for my school schedule, saving me time and money on transportation to classes. I am so glad that I learned this skill pre-pandemic, in addition to registering for these classes remotely and attending a workshop through the institution. This workshop happens in May of the school year before the scholarships are rewarded, so if you are a high school student and know where you will be attending in the fall, call up the institution and ask if they offer these types of workshops before attendance. You will be ahead of the game for the upcoming school year.

A faculty member runs this workshop. It is usually someone in the financial aid department. They walk you through the full process. You can also fill out an application online on your institution's website. Once the application is submitted, you are placed into a pot of potential scholarships for the entire institution based on your demographics. These scholarships are funded by multiple foundations, usually by graduates of a college or institution. If they do not offer this workshop, someone in financial aid can direct you to where you can apply for these institutional scholarships and grants. The thing about this is that you have no idea which type of scholarship you will be awarded or how much money you will receive. You may qualify for a grant or scholarship. You never know. I received $750 for this scholarship. The workshop took about an hour of my time.

The Gap Scholarship

This was the first scholarship I received, and it was my gateway drug. When I found out I had received this money, I was speechless. I received this before I knew about the appeal process described in the federal grants section. This scholarship is awarded to students who do not qualify for federal or state assistance because they work one or two jobs while attending school. Remember, Uncle Sam is watching you and how much money you claim on your tax return. This scholarship is based solely on that to "fill in the gap." I received $750 for this scholarship. This is one of the institutional scholarships I applied for through the workshop I attended. It took only one hour of my time. I recommend attending this workshop every year. Also, keep your eyes and ears peeled around your institution or university for other grant and scholarship opportunities. Have multiple conversations with student services employees, financial aid advisors, academic counselors, and librarians. When you start doing this, you will be able to determine whether applying for certain grant and scholarship opportunities is worth your time.

Bernie Moreno Scholarship

You might be thinking, "Who the hell is Bernie Moreno?" He is a successful local entrepreneur and alumni who started a foundation and donated funds to the institution where I received my bachelor's degree. This type of funding is a wonderful way to research independent foundational grants that are not funded by your local institution, particularly for graduate schools. The people who have these "non-profit" organizations are getting a tax deduction. For every dollar that they contribute to your education, they get to reduce the amount of money that they are contributing to taxes on their tax returns.

Again, this is a scholarship I received by filling out one form. This put me into a lottery for all the institutional grants that were available. I filled out this form in May of the previous academic year to be eligible for the following year. Have you noticed that I have not written an essay for any grants or scholarships that I have received? I received $3,000 for this scholarship.

2-for-1 Book Store Credit Award Scholarship

This scholarship was for $150 and had to be used directly in my institution's bookstore. Since Amazon has the most cost-efficient book prices, I used this scholarship for other things I needed or wanted. I received this during the pandemic. Even though we may not see another pandemic in this lifetime, it is helpful to know that these funds are available if you run into a roadblock. Let us say that you need to order a book, and the only way you can think of to pay for it is by putting it on your credit card with a high interest rate. Before you do that, call your institution's student services center, student accounts, or financial aid office to see if they have any funding available for students who require book funds. Do your research first. Go to the bookstore and find out how much the book you need costs, taxes and all. You can also make a quick phone call if you need it immediately and will not be on campus. Then, you are prepared with an answer if someone from your institution asks how much you need.

Joseph W. and Martha Peek Endowment Scholarship

I received this scholarship of $508 because there was a clerical error in my student account. The lesson here is to keep an eye on your student account. This is a great habit to get into, anyway. Banks make clerical errors all the time, and sometimes they can work out in your favor. What happened was that my institution took funds from my account before they were available. Since this was their mistake, they took money from another institution's foundation to cover the mistake. I know someone else who received a bank error in her favor. She received a $5,000 scholarship.

Caring Hearts Foundation Grant

When I entered graduate school, I realized that I was going to have to produce new ways to make money because I was no longer receiving Federal Pell Grant money. I received an email through my school email that was advertising a seasonal company looking for student employees to make passive income. This turned out to be fraud. I reported the scam to the campus police and informed student accounts and financial aid. This conversation was turned over to the dean of admissions. It was time consuming, but in the end, it was worth it. They decided that because it came through the student email system, the institution was responsible. They rewarded me with $1,067 from an institutional foundation that grants money to students in these types of scenarios. I highly recommend tapping into this resource when you are a student in need. You never know when you will need this tip.

Other Academic Financial Aid (That Did Not Work Out for Me)

These are other conventional ways in which people choose to make money while going through school that did not work out for me. I am not saying these ways will not work for you, but for my goal of *not trading hours for dollars,* these ways did not work.

Work/Study (Federal Aid Program)

I applied for and interviewed for a work/study position in the Student Services office. There are many work/study positions available through educational institutions. This position was hourly. They pay the federal minimum wage, which, when I applied, was $8.15 per hour. I should not have applied, but sometimes, I need to go through a process to find out that something is not for me, and you should too. You can qualify for a certain amount of hours and aid. Once that aid amount is fulfilled, you no longer have the job. If you do what I have instructed you to do and succeed in receiving a full Federal Pell Grant, you will not qualify for Federal Work/Study, and that is a good thing. Do you want more time devoted to your studies, more free time to do other things you enjoy, and receive over $6,895 for one trip to the financial aid office? Or do you want to make minimum wage and trade hours for dollars? You decide. Some people like it because they like getting paid to do their homework. That means you will spend that time at school when you could be studying in the comfort of your own home. You are also being interrupted all the time when you are doing work/studying and are not fully concentrating on schoolwork. Not for me.

It is always up to you how you want to spend your time. The power is in your hands.

Peer Tutor

I was hired in graduate school while working through my MBA program to be a peer tutor. They were paying $15 an hour. I thought this might work out because it was a remote position. The job required me to direct students to support services within the university. Again, this was a work/study position, where I could work on my schoolwork while being paid. I did not like the idea of being interrupted all the time, as I have read that it is not great for your mental health, but I figured I could work through that for the short term. I also had two weeks of training, with no light at the end of the tunnel. I was falling behind in my classes. In the interview process, I was told that I could work a maximum of 32 hours per week. I fantasized about what I could do with that money. Invest it? Work on other grant or scholarship applications? But after two weeks of training, there was no end in sight. I asked the people who hired me how long the training program was, and they would not give me a straight answer, so I quit. Focusing on my education was more important to me. Plus, why would I work for $15 per hour when I have a bachelor's degree? I made a little over $480 off this mistake.

My academic mentor said his six children were peer tutors during their school tenure. They were all math tutors. This enabled them to become better employees and better at math. There is always room for more math tutors at colleges, institutions, and universities, so if this is a strength of yours and you are planning on going into a math-related field, this is an excellent skill to have. Teaching and training others on what you know is a transferable skill to the workforce. Employers are always looking for ways to duplicate their stellar employees.

The MOS App

This is a national organization based in San Francisco. They have since converted to an app on your phone and offer banking services, both of which are beneficial for today's college students. They assign you to a scholarship counselor who helps match you with scholarships and grants. Mine was very friendly. I did not discover this service until I was well into my bachelor's/baccalaureate degree and had most of it paid for, so you may get better luck and results earlier in your academic career. I applied for several scholarships that pertained to my demographics but received nothing, not even a rejection letter, or a confirmation that they received my application. For me, this was a big waste of time. My counselor also referred me to the Peer Tutor position and kept framing it as a "grant" because it was Federal work/study money. This is not what I consider a grant. This is a job where you are trading hours for dollars. Again, not my cup of tea.

Grants & Scholarships I Received That Did Not Pertain to Getting a Degree

Before I enrolled in school full time, I was a full-time yoga teacher. I started by consistently practicing Bryan Kest's Power Yoga class for five years in Los Angeles, California. I paid for a 200-hour teacher training held by one of his predecessors. After I moved back home to Ohio, I became a full-time yoga teacher. Later, I wanted to do a Bryan Kest workshop at a local yoga studio to update my skills. I emailed the studio owner to let her know I wanted to attend the workshop. I included in my email that I was wondering if they had any opportunities for grants or scholarships.

I also offered cleaning services around the studio in exchange for the workshop. I had worked at a local yoga studio in Ukiah, California, and they let me take unlimited yoga classes whenever I wanted for free, as long as I would clean the studio for them two hours per week. This is where I got the idea. The owner emailed the next day, offering a full scholarship to the Bryan Kest workshop! I did not have to do anything in exchange. Remember, I only sent one email. I did not have to do anything except ask. This was a $150 value. If you get an opportunity like this or receive any other type of grant or scholarship, I recommend writing a thank-you letter to the foundation of the grant or scholarship you receive.

The second time, I received a fully funded 300-hour teaching training program. I was working at a few different yoga studios. One of my colleagues was putting together a teacher training program. We had talked briefly about working together on a partner yoga workshop. We promised to stay connected. He put me on his mailing list, and I received an email a few weeks later. He was advertising registration for his 300-hour Yoga Teacher Training certification. The training was valued at over $3,000. It ran every Saturday for fourteen weeks. I mentally started rearranging my schedule. I wanted to do this training to get certified at the 300-hour level. This would allow me to obtain the highest level of certification for a yoga teacher.

I immediately emailed the teacher and asked if he needed anyone to do administrative work for his upcoming program in exchange for a full scholarship to the training program. (This was before I had an MBA, so I had no idea what administrative tasks would involve.) He texted me soon after and agreed to my offer. We met for coffee and discussed the details and duties. In that meeting, he said that, right before he sent out the email to advertise the teacher training, he was speaking to his wife and asked her, "How am I going to find someone to do this administration stuff?" The next day, I emailed him and made my request, so it was a perfect match! Remember, all I had to do was ask, and it was given.

This teacher training was also a lifelong dream of mine. During those fourteen weeks, I created a disclaimer agreement and had other people sign it who had paid for the training. I transcribed seminar recordings, which allowed the training to seep deeper into my subconscious. I applied to the National Yoga Alliance for the process of starting a nonprofit and getting the program certified by this alliance, which was the national recognition at the time. I also lost about fifteen pounds during a three-part community-supported cleanse, received the certification that I wanted, and made lifelong friends in the process. The administrative services I offered were well worth the benefits of the program.

While writing this book, I decided to take a break and reward my fingers for the first nine pages by going to my local nail salon and getting a manicure. While waiting for my technician to wrap up her last customer, I noticed a bulletin-board posting in the lobby area. It was advertising complimentary ballroom dance lessons and a feature on *Dancing with the Stars* at a local dance studio. I had recently been thinking about signing up for dance lessons, so I called the number on the flier to see if they had fulfilled the advertisement. I spoke with the owner/choreographer for a few minutes, and he said I was a "perfect fit" for what they were looking for. I told him I was a full-time student and had previously taken dance lessons in swing, salsa, tango, and ballet. I had always wanted to learn ballroom dancing. They were also looking for someone who would like to promote their business or non-profit organization. I told them I was writing an eBook I would like to promote. I have to provide my dance shoes, and the dance studio will provide costumes, videography, choreography, and a height-appropriate dance partner. I start next week!

Other Social Programs I Used

Medicaid & EBT Program

This section is a bonus because these are not grants or scholarships, but they are social programs that assisted me in getting through college as a full-time student. I realized while I was writing this book that I was able to capitalize on getting some of these grants because I had access to Medicaid (medical care) and the EBT program (Supplemental Nutrition Program). Both programs are nationally recognized, and you can access them throughout your county. I received both of them together. The name of the offices in my geographical area is (County name) Job and Family Services. You do have to prove your status as a full-time student and your income level to receive these benefits and renew them every year. It is well worth it. There were many times during my college tenure when I was grateful for both. It alleviated the health problems I had that I was putting off for years. If you are under twenty-six, check to see if you are still covered with health insurance by your parents if you do not know.

Project Go!

One of the institutions I attended had a program called Project Go! It may be called something else in your institution. This program supports full-time students in getting discounts for their utility bills and offers grants when they cannot pay their rent. It is well worth looking into when you are in a bind. You can access this program through your financial aid and student services offices.

Donate Plasma

This program is not for everyone. You can make between $3,000 and $5,000 per year. If you can bear having a needle stuck in your arm and do not mind dealing with the scar, you can take advantage of this program. These plasma centers are built in low-income areas and are often on college campuses. Plasma is white blood cells. The plasma center uses a machine to separate your white and red blood cells and return your red blood cells to you, along with a saline return to replace the white blood cells they took. Initially, the donation process is a bit time consuming. The first time I donated, it took almost five hours, but they greatly reward new donors. I went to a terribly busy donation center. They put you through a rigorous physical. They check your vitals, and you have to be healthy to donate. The staff checks your blood pressure, protein, temperature, and iron levels every time you donate. You may go twice per week to donate, and you are helping someone who has an immune deficiency. This is where white blood cells are distributed. They put your payment funds on a Visa gift card, and you can also acquire reward points towards travel and more cash. It is a great program that helps a lot of people. Look into it by Googling your local plasma donation center. This is also a remarkable thing to put on your resume under volunteering.

How to Know if a Grant or Scholarship is Right For You

I hope that this eBook has been useful to you. I have applied for many more grants and scholarships that did not come to fruition, so if you want to get the same results I did, target these specific scholarships and grants, if they pertain to your demographic. If I did this again, I would not apply for external scholarships outside my institution. They were a waste of time.

For instance, I applied for an Ayn Rand scholarship after a lecture that my economics professor gave. I applied for the scholarship after reading her books, like *Atlas Shrugged*. But after applying and receiving a rejection letter, I discovered that there were thousands of applicants. Realizing how many applicants there were showed me that the chances of winning that scholarship were ridiculously small. I am talking a 0.00001% chance. A terrific way to gauge whether you have a chance of winning is if you are speaking to someone who can tell you what the chances are. Submitting a scholarship essay into a vast oblivion will not get you the grant or scholarship. It is unlikely you will get a response back. The same goes for job applications.

If you are reading the grant or scholarship requirements, and you personally do not fit into the demographics that the scholarship is looking for, there is no point in applying. For example, I attended an institutional scholarship workshop, and one caught my eye that a woman who was running the workshop was telling me about. When I read the qualifications, you needed to be under the age of twenty-six.

All of the other demographics I fit into, but I was older than twenty-six. Yes, this is age discrimination for a scholarship. Not to worry, there are plenty of grants and scholarships out there for every different kind of person, from disabled veterans to single mothers.

If You Do Decide to Take Out Loans

There is a document that everyone must sign if they decide to take out loans called a *Master Promissory Note*. If you do decide to take out loans, please be sure to read it very carefully, so that you know what your responsibilities are and are not on the other side of your education. Somewhere between your graduation date and six months from that date, someone from the financial services where you took your loans out will call you to discuss how you want to pay your loans. They will discuss with you how much you want to pay per month on your school loans. On your MPN, it says that you have to pay a minimum of $50 per month. There is currently a law in place that says after 25 years, your student loans will be forgiven. It is called The Student Loan Forgiveness Act, which was put in place by President Barack Obama during his presidency in 2012. You will receive more loan forgiveness if you get full Pell Grant funding. The steps I provided in the Federal Funding section will support you with this. You can do the math on how much you will actually pay over a lifetime if you pay the minimum (studentaid.gov).

Conclusion

I believe that this book will be handy throughout your undergraduate tenure. I received the majority of my funding during that time. It will save you a ton of time and money. I contend that it is well worth the price of this eBook. If you take my advice and receive a grant or scholarship, it will easily pay for the cost of this book. Not only can you finish this book in one evening, but you can also keep it as a handbook for future reference. If you enjoyed this book and have received a grant or scholarship from what I have shared, please refer this title to your classmates, colleagues, professors, or relatives entering or reentering college life. I would appreciate it, and they will appreciate you.

Gratitude

Much gratitude goes out to the team of people that made this book possible. In no particular order:

To my editor, Mike Dell, for his speed and professionalism for getting this project complete.

To Valentina, who designed my book cover, for her professionalism, skill, and aligning with my vision and revisions so quickly.

To Tammy, who wrote my book description, and made me cry with joy after utilizing her writing skills. I felt seen.

To my business partner, Dr. Carl Collins, for his ongoing belief and support of me to complete and further my education beyond my wildest dreams, when no one else would. In addition, for his legal coaching, and making me a priority when I needed him to stay in my corner.

To all of the foundations mentioned in this book, who gave me the money to complete my education. This book and my education would not have been possible without all of your contributions.

To all of the present and future college students or parents of college students, who bought this book as a guide to pay for college. Thank you for your support.

References

Federal Student Aid. (2024, May 13). *How much money can I get from a federal Pell Grant?* https://studentaid.gov/help-center/answers/article/how-much-money-can-i-get-federal-pell-grant

Federal Student Aid. (2023, August 5). U.S. Department of Education. https://studentaid.gov/manage-loans/forgiveness-cancellation/debt-relief-info.

IRS. (2023, January 31). CARES Act Coronavirus Relief Fund frequently asked questions. https://www.irs.gov/newsroom/cares-act-coronavirus-relief-fund-frequently-asked-questions

Kasich, J. R. (2024, May 13). *2017 minimum wage.* Ohio Department of Commerce Division of Industrial Compliance. https://com.ohio.gov/static/documents/dico_2017MinimumWageposter.pdf

Krupnick, M. (2022, February 10). *US universities: More college students are dropping out during Covid. It could get worse.* https://www.theguardian.com/us-news/2022/feb/10/college-students-dropout-covid-pandemic

Made in the USA
Coppell, TX
08 February 2025

45580764R00025